PRAISE FOR the lake-shaped excuse

"In striking lines that repeat and mirror in fractals, these poems tease out memory like a prayer, capturing the pain and claustrophobia of sudden loss: 'My mother's name is mine and buried in my throat.' From the book's meditative opening, Clayton beautifully voices an embodied experience of grief and its visceral pleading: 'I already have / every memory of / you I ever will.' What a gift to encounter a book that recognizes how the death of a mother gnaws from within – and to be guided so tenderly through its testimony of love."

– **CASSIDY MCFADZEAN**, author of *Crying Dress*

"*the lake-shaped excuse* is brilliant and painful. Conyer Clayton takes us deep into grief's interior, where a mother's absence becomes a vital presence, carried not only in memory but in voice and body – 'My head is her head and / her aura mine.' Tender yet unflinching, these poems grapple with illness, addiction, violence and regret. Yet they return, again and again, to the daily practice of loving – through acts of imagination, friendship, nature and sobriety – because ultimately 'connection / is the window / of wanting I want / to look through // the lake I want / to stand in.'"

– **MIKKO HARVEY**, author of *Let the World Have You*

"[A] beautiful, thoughtful, insightful and elegiac collection . . . grapples with grief so thoroughly and so brazenly and so beautifully that you, like, finish reading it and you realize that you haven't exhaled since page two. The collection is gorgeous and difficult and thoughtful and it really shows that Clayton is a poetic force to be reckoned with."

– **KATE SIKLOSI** and **DANI SPINOSA** of Gap Riot Press on "Kneeling in Our Name"

"The hauntingly beautiful poems in Conyer Clayton's *the lake-shaped excuse* are appropriately ripple-like in their transmutational, incantatory quality. Echoes of the speaker's mother's voice resound and are made new through the speaker's own voice, resulting in a kind of blood harmony utterly unique to genetic passage. The mother and the speaker are not the same person, but in many ways, of course they are, such is 'the terrible unity of wanting.' These poems want against absence, they reach for what is no longer there . . . but still they reach anyway. This body of work, like a body of water, refuses stagnation – this is a project born of an ever-expanding love that gives life to grief and asks, 'What if / (another expanding tear) / But how,' in the same paradoxical breath. There is real music behind these quiet devotions, and we're warmly, generously invited to listen closely. May we all learn to practice patience and grace in the face of grief, connection in the face of loss. May we trust in what lies beyond ourselves. 'Pray. Then / start again.'"

– **CHELSEA HARLAN**, author of *Bright Shade*

the lake-shaped excuse

ALSO BY CONYER CLAYTON

But the sun, and the ships, and the fish, and the waves.

We Shed Our Skin Like Dynamite

the lake-shaped excuse

poems

conyer clayton

A Buckrider Book

Published by Buckrider Books
an imprint of Wolsak and Wynn Publishers
280 James Street North
Hamilton, Ontario L8R 2L3
www.wolsakandwynn.ca

Editor for Buckrider Books: Paul Vermeersch | Editor: Natasha Ramoutar |
Copy editor: Ashley Hisson
Cover and interior design: Natalie Olsen
Author photograph: Joanna Eldredge Morrissey
Typeset in Erato
Printed by Coach House Printing Company, Toronto, Canada

The publisher gratefully acknowledges the support of the Canada Council for the Arts and the Ontario Arts Council. We also acknowledge the financial support of the Government of Canada through the Canada Book Fund and the Government of Ontario through the Ontario Book Publishing Tax Credit and Ontario Creates.

LIBRARY AND ARCHIVES CANADA CATALOGUING IN PUBLICATION

Title: the lake-shaped excuse / Conyer Clayton.
Names: Clayton, Conyer, author.
Identifiers: Canadiana 20260240869 | ISBN 9781998408504 (softcover)
Subjects: LCGFT: Poetry.
Classification: LCC PS8605.L395 L35 2026 | DDC C811/.6—dc23

for the best mommy in the whole wide world

This world is what everyone should get down on their knees for.
My mother, asleep on her left side.

– MARTA BALCEWICZ –

Big Shadow

contents

STANDING

Day of rest

a devoted congregation gathers
between my wrists and I slap them

down the vents
there is a golden bell ringing

in the hollow of my throat
sonorous, pendulous, 11:00 a.m.

no one hears it
no one hears me

shush me, musty
when I am all fours

on the carpet every morning
preparing to swing

threading the needle
greasing my metal

testing if my rib cage
peels back against the petals

or not, if a damaged
nerve threatens

to pinch, or not
I pray

no one will open the gate
climb the ladder

swing us open
hit me

kneeling

Your smile comes running at me like a
herd down a hill, milk down the chin.

You make me think of death.

– **URSULA ANDKJÆR OLSEN** –
Third-Millennium Heart,
translated by Katrine Øgaard Jensen

Kneeling in our name

i.

I've never
wanted anything

except for someone
to understand

I actually want
many things

little green leaves
severed
by time and tension

my mouth closed
our name
our wanting

a dry
window

the carpet
a body
a lake

the terrible unity of wanting
and
the refusal to express it

ii.

Browned edges.
Water droplets

on the corners
of the windows

I wipe
like a sermon.

Every day
like a sermon.

The temperature
drops.

I kneel
to stretch my neck.

Every day
like a sermon

I kneel
to stretch my neck.

Like a prayer to
something

I don’t believe
in –

a body
without
pain

a body
that
will heal

with
my wanting
(only me
only mine)

a body
without
someone’s
wanting

a life
without
giving
my body

iii.

Every day. Water
droplets on my edges.
I dab my face
with oil, shove
Vaseline into my
nostrils. Every day.
I want to erase
some years.
Kneeling pain.
Water wanting.
A clear vision
of leaves looking
through the dry
window. A lake
with no water
and me at the centre
kneeling wanting
nothing. Water
nothing. Kneeling
leaves. Pointing.
What do you want?
What is your name?
A small gift like
a prayer given
to me in ink.
A cold window.
A warm want.
Our name once
gave me

nothing but
want and refusal

then concession
now connection

and connection
is the window
of wanting I want
to look through

the lake I want
to stand in

the water I wish
to drown in

but I wipe it
off instead.

iv.

My mother's name is mine and buried in my throat.
Her name is buried in my throat.
You scratch at her when you call to me.
When I kneel on the carpet.
When I stretch my neck to reach her.
When I reach into my throat to touch her.
I said our name so many times my voice was abandoned
in the water. She signed her own name
and the ink became a window.
In this window I am kneeling, reflected, mouthing
my own name. Like a prayer.
The temperature drops. The dead freeze
in the throat of the voiceless.
Living made timeless when she smiles.
The pain? Right here.
Pointing. Always in my throat.

v.

My throat is a shitty chain restaurant, yellow queso, under
ripe tomatoes. Tostitos, cinnamon rolls, Jack and water.
Bourbon and ginger, Everclear and OJ. My throat

is *your turn*, white ceiling, white window, coffee mug,
brown wood, riding a bus as the sun comes up, riding
a bus next to clear water, a sincere hug, *nice to meet you*,

blood in the shower water. My voice is her eyes blank
and shiny years later when I told her how it happened,
when I repeated myself, my voice is me not wanting

to repeat myself because my voice is tired, because
her eyes are blank and shiny, because she does not
understand (no, she understands too well).

Her mind is a photo I find, the photo I show her, she
didn't mean for me to see it. Her body is tired
and locked in the bathroom but she rubs my eyes

regardless, lays with her legs intertwined in mine.
Her voice is whispering while I rub her back, full of
questions I should have asked but now her voice is gone,

and mine. Her body is

pulled to the side of the road, waiting for her aura to pass,
in bed, for the seizure to stop, and my body is kneeling
on the bathroom floor with her, blood on

the concrete, blood on the tile, blood on my brand-new
shirt and ten staples to her head. My head is her head and
her aura mine, light the same light the same waiting

the same wanting the same sleeping the same drink
pouring. My lungs are a cracked window, her soft hands,
she sat with me every day. Every day

to fix the straps on my face, can't breathe Mom
can't breathe.

Our hurt is kneeling on the carpet, in front of the toilet,
in front of the man, in front of the bed, in the back
of the mirror.

Our voice is   unremembering

the prayer of our kneeling, the hushed harsh redness of
our skin. My voice is quiet, we were sleeping for so long.
Right here, it hurts right here when I talk about it,

pointing, the muscles, it doesn't matter how I kneel, who
I kneel to, where I paddle, the water won't flush it away,
the sunlight the acid the burning his eyes, the pills I took

from those strangers those times.

When I was left
at the after-party,
she picked me up,
when she cried
in the big big bed,
I picked her up,

when we drowned in the after eyes,
when she said those words to me,

when love
when love
when love,

every day.

But I couldn't do a damn thing to help. It hurt
right here, pointing, right here, kneeling,
right here, still.

vi.

I take the pill they tell me to
thirty minutes before two meals a day.
They send a camera
down my throat
to assess the state of my esophagitis
every six months.

What's left living of you in me.

My voice was once the loudest in the room
and now no one can hear me.

Your laugh was once the loudest in the room.

My throat's already red and getting redder.
Every day. It's red and getting redder.

Everyone says I laugh like you.

vii.

I eat only oatmeal.
No milk on my chin.
Plain tofu.
Nothing red.

Sometimes I forget
your smile

my body
thinks only red
thinks thick
thinks stiff
tough
rejects my efforts

viii.

Your smile makes me think of death because
you are dead

and this fact, is it
making me red?

Your deadness unable to
verify facts, reduce their
swelling.

If you were less dead you'd rub
my eyes to sleep

If you were less dead I'd wipe
the milk from your chin
the crackers
the peanut butter
from your collar

ix.

sometimes when I'm kneeling
if you were less dead
like a prayer
through a clear dry window
into a clear clear lake
into the spaces
between previously conjoined
leaves

I mouth

you were so good   to me   and all this

is really
sticky for me   really real

did it happen
that way   like that   or   am I did I am I

red

what was sticky
for you

why didn't I
ask
if you were red then too
why did I do
anything but
even now   are we
red together still
together in your smile
together, red
tomorrow, red
forever, red
and wanting,
red and living,
beautifully red, it's

milk you're
supposed to drink
they say
but it doesn't work
for me
only facts
and I can't have them
only water
and I can't stand in it

only photographs, dead
memory, falling alone from the chair
in the closet, reaching for something, cracking

a rib, looking for me
through the window, still smiling
as you tell me
how it happened.

x.

Every day. Water droplets on my edges. I dab my face with oil, shove Vaseline into my nostrils. Every day. I want to erase some years. **Kneeling** pain. Water wanting. A clear vision of leaves looking **through the dry window**. A lake with no water and me at the center kneeling wanting nothing. Water nothing. Kneeling leaves. Pointing. What do you want? What is your name? A small gift like a prayer given to me in ink. A cold window. A warm want. our name once gave me nothing but want and refusal then concession now connection and connection is the window of **wanting** I want to look through the lake I want to stand in the water I wish **to drown** in but I wipe it off **instead**.

to drown instead

wanting

Every day. Water droplets on my edges. I dab my face with oil, shove Vaseline into my nostrils. Every day. I want to **erase** some years. Kneeling pain. Water **wanting**. A clear vision of leaves looking through the dry window. A lake with **no** water and me at the centre kneeling **wanting** nothing. Water nothing. Kneeling leaves. Pointing. What do you want? What is your name? A small gift like a prayer given to me in ink. A cold window. A warm **want**. Our name once gave me **nothing** but **want** and refusal then concession now connection and connection is the window of **wanting** I want to look through the lake I want to stand in the water I wish to drown in but I wipe it off instead.

erase
wanting
no wanting

want.
nothing. want
wanting
wish instead

xi.

Every day. Water droplets on my edges. I dab my face with oil, shove Vaseline into my nostrils. **Every day**. I want to erase some years. Kneeling pain. Water wanting. A clear vision of leaves looking through the dry window. A lake with no water and me at the center kneeling wanting nothing. Water nothing. Kneeling leaves. Pointing. **What do you want?** What is your name?

A small gift like a prayer given to me in ink. A cold window. A warm want. our name once gave me **nothing but** want and refusal then concession now connection and connection is the window of wanting I want to look through the lake I want **to stand** in the water I wish to drown in but I wipe it off instead.

floating

Silence and writing are, if not quite the same thing,
then allies – each a misdirection of the unspeakable,
and each a way of holding on.

– MIRIAM TOEWS –

A Truce That Is Not Peace

My little sister asks me

after Sanna Wani's "Lately I am Trying"

if I remember when I realized I could die and I don't, but I wish I did. Did I even think as a child? Do I even think now? So much of my world develops like a photograph, in the dark room way back and is fully formed before I realize it has been there floating in chemicals I assembly-line walk by. If I think in words, I don't know them. If I knew I could die, I was okay with it. I tell my sister I feel like I have no memory sometimes – I spit shine my own eyes so they'll see something. The snow I forgot was falling. The ice I walked on weeks too early. If I realized I could die, I don't remember it. It's not my death that worries me. It's yours. If my lake isn't solid, maybe yours is. Yours is. Yours is. No one else can die because the ice is just a photograph I took in high school. I made you sit on a pool noodle in the middle of the street while I crouched to get an artsy angle. Your skirt was striped and black and white. I think I need to go home.

Chaudière Falls

I can never remember the difference between ligaments
and tendons. It all has to do with what you're attached to.
Liquid slipping

over rocks. The sound of water is the same
as silence. What oils surface when I settle

and sense nothing over the drone?
No crepitus, lubrication – things
only heard, not felt. I could almost

believe I'm brand-new, in the making,
just emerging like a swell that fell far
below the white high-water mark
on the dam where splash survives.

The top ridge is already drying
even though the sun is weak today.

It's not even noon and already
I can tell the day is over.

Signs spell out danger but they only draw me nearer.
The older the staircase the looser the joint.

I move my knees in tiny circles every time

the horizon brightens.
The moment I woke up,

I heard something.

The ropy fascia of my happiness connects
to the bone of quiet.

Is that how these things work again?
My mood is aching.

Close your eyes so you can see

Sunset
the   countdown

smudged
against my eyelids

doom stencilled in
permanent

marker on yellow
fading light.

Why are you shaking
little leg?

You're nervous, you're tired, you're
     already exhausted just thinking about

how your actual strength
fails you.

Another warning?
Another scar

          on what ought to be
hopeful, the biggest muscle group

     in the body
     the biggest body
     in the galaxy

kept warm
by its own refusal to take part
in the end

we know is coming.
It's coming.

The tear / The day

you forget to listen
because bodies
remember

harm past healing

and the sun
remembers

its own birth, something
   we've been spared.

The boom is etched
in its magmatic memory, simmering

waiting.   So you close your eyes against it.

You bask in the false summer
of a sunlit patch
in mid-winter.

Who walks away clean

I hunker lower
into the wet spot behind
my liver and avoid

admissions of guilt.

I may have been a brat then but

I was embedded
in futon cushions
too deep

to see myself frowning,

paperclips twisted
and caked in black resin.

I'm trying

to scrape this clean   not smoke it

  pack it loosely   let some air in.

I've reused my body
until it can't help but

                    scatter

on the carpet.

Even vacuums don't reach.

Tough bristle –
                    my mother.

My mother
taught me baking soda.

My mother taught me not
to take this
but she took it

and I did too.

A fly lands on the window

He crawls and vomits
on the sky itself,

digesting the horizon
before it can be revealed.

Replacement therapy

I let myself be hungry too long.
The mild discomfort a nail to bite,   filed dust
of my own body, scattered.   /   My sand dunes
everywhere / scent / hair / spit / snail trail on
the front of his jeans.

I notch this existence as mine.   (*check check*)

If I feel no burn,   I have no fire.
So I nibble or not.
Gnaw / pick / fester / embodied / scolded –

Stop that.

Don't look away.

A shell picked up on the beach.
(*Why that one?*)

It's the same as the others / cracked ridge
small grey mountain in stormwater
churned – cum / beer / vomit / bong water
float at the surface or

sink to the bottom. (*you can see this from space*)

What swims between the dead things
inhabits the core where currents don't reach / rot caught
in an industrial net

(*this isn't what we cast for*)
bottle caps
dolphins mixed with carp
seaweed tangles

What just touched me?

It's not the dead things we fear

but a quick life

that grazes our calves.

Coral is fragile / My oils rub off and kill
entire ecosystems / little guppy nips
little notecards / jot calories / gulp

my shrinking stomach (*clumsy*)

Fins fumble.
Let hunger edge
you (*sick pride*)

At least it's something.

Maybe my horoscope was right /

Maybe I do need drama – instability

keeps the gummy linings taut /

soul to smoke

blackness to booze /

periphery

/

purging

Carry on

A limb becomes
increasingly heavy
once numb.

A spleen stuffed
into a suitcase will overstretch
the seams. The zipper catches.

A piece is
missing
left

somewhere, kicked
around on tile. Quiet

danger of a different
body. Quiet danger
of your own.

Once punctured always punctured.
Your body is an origami.
The tube rolls its eyes in your chest.

How easily we unfold
and no one taught us
the pattern. The paper

blooms in my hands, bloody
and wetting and
wetting and ripped

What if

(another expanding tear)

But how

Perennial

i. grieving, year 10

I already have
every memory of
you I ever will.

ii.

But there is regret
and a fear of regret
and an anticipation
of inevitable regret
I regret and regret
the fear of regret
yet there is still
regret inevitable
regret there
is a regret
and fear
of
it

But there is regret
and a fear of regret
and an anticipation
of inevitable regret
I regret and regret
the fear of regret
yet there is still
regret inevitable
regret there
is a regret
and fear
of
it

iii. grieving, year 12

a mother   not
  in my life

laughs

iv.

There is a man with a stone inside him. When they cut him open on the autopsy table, the stone fills the sky, covers the horizon of memory. Cause of death: stone. But it was the stone keeping him alive, his skin together, the patterns of his life clear. They cannot understand. Too big for the body does not mean too big. Leaving the body does not mean leaving.

v.

my mom
buried

alive under
Ritz crackers
peanut butter

mortar

vi. grieving, year 8

Maybe no one
will ever find her

urn at the bottom of the lake.

Some guppy will make its home there.
Crux of the (un)natural world –

snakes unhinge their jaws in tribute
to future generations.

Whole valleys spill over with orgies
of ants and sparrows; the swarming
fruits birthed in an afterlife.

Centipedes scramble
to have their future told.

Tell me what I already know:

The grass never grows there again.
The grass will never grow there again.

I don’t know
how long ago that tree tipped over

marked the spot
we stopped

agreed
waded in

and
emptied

her body slowly
into the water

In the box of jewellery we went through when our mother died

there were many gold-hoop earrings but none of them
matching.

There was a gold watch, and pearls, and a ring
with our birthstones.

There was a gold-coin necklace she wore almost daily.

I draped it over the box where her urn lived –
the back of a shelf by the bathroom.

This was the degree of visibility
I could manage in those early months.

I only wanted to display what she'd chosen
to show the world,
remember

her neck, glinting
and sparkly. I think

an old friend stole the necklace and sold it for cocaine.
My mother's memory became something to crush
and snort, coin for coin.

I cried telling my sisters that I'd lost
what they trusted me with.
That I lost trust in who I trusted.

Encasement

Because you were given to me when I wanted you gone, I felt I owned you.

Because I saw a concrete box enter a furnace but never your body, I owned what was left of it.

Because I wish for your body, and regret that wish, your body becomes both wish and regret.

Because I never saw your body, I own it and your falling.

You don't drift, lifted ember. You wanted to. I think I remember you said that once. Fly off. Pond scum. Heart. You said that once.

I want to be the lake where you were happy. I could own you happy there. I could own your body happy there. I could be pond scum there with you, happy.

I touched the water once and you floated on top. I could own your float. Even this wish, resistant.

Because I'll never own you happy, your float, your fly, I clutch to owning your ashes, to doing what I will.

Because you sat on my bookshelf between pictures of us for nearly eight years, I grew heavy and uncomfortable.

Because you lived so solid right in front of my bed, because I cannot think of you and not your ashes, because I cannot not own them. Because I cannot not see them sit like a trinket, among the other trinkets I own, and rocks I pick as souvenirs.

Things to remember. Concrete box and box and fire. Things to remember. What feels right in my palm.

When you catch my eye in dreams, I cannot remember you warm in my hand.

Cloud cover

someone tries
to forget
something

It was the first day of the year warm enough to swim so we did

There are spots in the lake so cold I can't believe it. Still, they're surrounded by heat. I cried on a slick rock with my feet in the water. One stroke to the left, I'm warm again. The move from pleasure back to pain is just one quick kick away. A hand on my hip a small moment too long. That memory isn't even there, but my voice is gone again, gone again, gone again, gone.

Take a hand down from the sky. What a gentle hand. Just trying to help. But I need my own hand, my stupid hand, so stupid it won't even help until I stop calling it stupid. But it won't lift a damn finger. It's cramping up even now.

Crafting a lake-shaped excuse to bury me in.

Floating in our name

A lake with no water.

The centre		wanting nothing.

Water nothing. Water wanting.

Our voice the prayer of our kneeling,

A warm gift. A small want.

What do you want to erase some years.

What is mine and buried.

Once the loudest in the room.

Your laugh fills the room.

Your in the room

Everyone says I

laugh like you

Toad in the firepit

moved rocks
logs that blocked

and you left
without resistance

little red
lifted ember

sometimes
someone

is trying
to help you

standing

Forgive me for committing to suffering. I thought it might be the answer. That if I suffered loudly enough, for long enough, I would be owed something from somewhere holy.

– **HANIF ABDURRAQIB** –

There's Always This Year

Ode to silent mornings

good morning to the silent mornings.
maybe I'll speak today.

some days feel better
with silence but I don't know
that those around me agree.

my speech therapist asks me: *when was the last time you felt fully yourself?*

it's somehow both when I am alone and silent
and when I am surrounded by people, speaking.

I like to think my contradictions should be
sucked up by sunlight but really –
I just want less explaining of me.

//

good morning to the water in the lake
that's always there. let's go kayaking
and not talk about it –

every other sound in the world
is more interesting than me describing myself

again. let's just float
and know we are

hearing the same thing.

Ripple

I don't understand
I don't understand

the impulse to disturb
the impulse to disturb

still water

to skip rocks
to skip rocks

displacement
displacement

and destruction
and destruction

camouflaged
camouflaged

as craft

Today I put my hands into dirt, and it was warm

what a good day

My group chat asks me

about my dreams, and I have little to tell anymore. I used to wake at night and speak to myself. Now when I wake I stay silent. The dreambone connects to the voicebone. The voicebone connects to air. My physiotherapist taught me how to stretch it: You take the air between two fingers in one hand and push it flat under the palm of the other. You pull but not until it tears, that's how you got in this mess, only listening to dreams instead of silence. Voice is invisible until you notice its absence, and then you see nothing else. We fill our lungs with thirty pounds of air a day. I try and move my diaphragm from my lowest rib to my highest until I balloon and float away on air I've lengthened through months of dedicated daily practice. In a lucid dream, most people try to fly. I am not different, jetting my silent self from appointment to appointment. I hope my doctor is proud.

The mirror

decadence over the big blue couch   my mother's legacy   curling
gold frame   heavy beauty   all of us together in it   in every house
each move   contained   unending   we all
stand together   inside   we all stand together   smiling
in my memory   no matter who enters the picture
no matter   no matter
who leaves it

we are the four of us   smiling inside gold lattice   we are the four smiling
facing each other   we are side by side   facing each other

facing each other   we are side by side   facing each other
we are the four of us   smiling inside gold lattice   we are the four smiling

who leaves it

no matter   no matter

I don't know how it's possible

but I'm sober, and I can see the sun on my thumb.
Circle and spot. I mean I can see the sun's
reflection, on my thumb, twice over, through
my sunglasses and off the deck
and if I squint and tilt my head so the electric currents
run off me in waves
then I can smell it, the fusion, like a barbeque
on a dragonfly's eye. How many eyes
glint in each sunspot? I'd say the same number as solar
storms I'm tracking on just my right hand.
I can see it

and my vision persists, unpocked.
Even the sun has sheltered marks moving
across its lifescape.

My sobriety is an anomaly

much like a supernova in a mid-size star
that still has helium. I also stopped
before I imploded, much to the chagrin of your
hypothesis, the opposite of the scientific literature of rock
bottom, quaky magma
never stopped me from missing deadlines.

I swear this isn't a simile. I really stared at the sun today,
face down on the deck, and
you may not believe me, but I stopped drinking
when I was the happiest I've ever been, like the sun

and I'm done second-guessing myself
just because your theory charts alcoholism
on a jagged trajectory.

The sun and I, we're smooth, baby, we're sifting gold
over craters of cold.

Chipmunks

i.

My mom used to fall
around every distant corner
before I could call out to her.

the ragged verge of waking
the cliff edge in a recurring dream

I am awake.
I know what's there. I know
I can never get to it.

ii.

A shadow pulls
at the bottom right corner of my eye

frayed rug of my vision

iii.

I see chipmunks and say hello to my mom.

Once I said hello to a leaf
on the passenger seat of my car.

iv.

My mom saw auras and all
her daughters do too.

What floats in
our collective vision

that no one else can see.
Why can't we take

a solid look

v.

Tugging, falling, tripping
around the corner
of my awareness.

if it shuffles

if it stomps

if it never
disappears

Her armfuls of bread

How to resurrect her in print.

To sever
myself from experience.

How to make a syllable of her death

    and life – her
crispy onions and laugh.

I wish I'd write poems about the last time I saw her.

How many times I said I'm sorry.

I make a record of her typos – how we light up her life.

How I tried to write a poem in the sun and
it became her death.

How a phone call in Bangkok sent me sprawling
to the floor and vomiting in airports, resentfully
taking shots of sake and wishing someone would ask
what happened?

How long it took for the image in my head to become
her face

breaking into laughter
or chewing a cracker
or from that one day
I came over to do laundry
and she was sitting on the bed crying
how her face
just broke.

How her hair looked better curly.

//

Just now happy.
Opening her curtains.

//

After I shushed her in the theatre, she laid her head
on my shoulder, embarrassed.

I felt bad for ebbing her laughter and
touched the top of her head to let her know.

She had to have known.

She knew. Right?

Google Doc of Death

I created the shared Google Doc of Death tonight, a
random weekday evening. Earlier I stood by the river,
content. I wrote in the third person.
Conyer wants to be cremated. There's been
a storm coming for days now, but it never comes.
The wind just teases. Gusts. Holds seagulls still above
the water. *Conyer wants to be a birch, or maybe an oak, but*
probably a birch. Far away. There are so many blackbirds
hovering against grey clouds, they look like gnats, but
without reason. The air couldn't be thicker. You could
squeeze it, then little droplets, birds
would fall from the sky. *Conyer wants the rest of their ashes to*
be divided among those who want some, to do with what they will,
what would make them happy. There's a spot here we could
come and swim once the storm builds and breaks.
Water in all considerations. Submersion. Incoming.
Held aloft. The driest one could ever be.
Conyer wants to be cremated. The driest I could ever be.

Non-rechargeable D

My mom had a handful of tweezers.
She had several armfuls of bread.

I have a basketful of batteries
and they are dead, drained

by remotes and razors, flashlights,
but I only remember buying that one

size, a giant non-rechargeable D.
The man at the gas station seemed

impressed by its heft when he held it
out to me. I was impressed too, how it

weighed my purse down
the entire drive home.

Marble people

after Mary Ruefle's "A Morning Person"

I'm sitting on my porch and hating my own poems. Many of my closest friends live in other cities. In my poems, I only love myself. Off paper, I love my people so much I cry if I think about it too long.

Sometimes I lose myself in deathdreams. I fall or drop the phone. Go silent. Erase the memory entirely. I draft my automatic grief email response. I learn from past mistakes.

But in poems, I stomp to the front, and these people I love, they love me too – they let me come forward easily. They glide like marbles around me,

round and cold and smooth and kind. I love them so, their shiny humanness.

I might cry, thinking of myself among marbles who love me. I am in a dense sea of marbles, clattering gently against me. The sun gestures through the clouds.

It's June – wild chicory coughs up flowers on the lawn and my neighbour strolls by to harvest the purple blooms.

She is a marble among marbles and so am I, clinking against my coffee mug expectantly. *Good morning.*

Good morning. I'm finally not too busy to say hello. What will you use those flowers for?

Restful as a wasp

I forgot to tuck my legs away when I was done
with them. I'm a ladybug just landed, softwing

showing under hardwing, sheer
curtains under the blackout. Are we inside

or out, the window
or the screen, the trigger
or the memory – I'm done with it.

I'm coming in to land. I'll take a gap year
on a warm flat of brick, the twenty two-by-fours

under the deck. I'm the plastic
in the crawl space that refuses to be glued.

My wings no one sees, gather moisture.
There's water where there shouldn't be
but who made you the rock police, huh?

If my legs are slate, tired as granite, limestone
shaved or stubbly, that's fine by me.

Does escape take place
within my body
or without it, wither my body
or with him. I dare you

to rest with some uncertainty
for a full calendar year. Double-dog.
Triple-bee. I quadruple-demon dare you

to not make plans except stretching.
Make your body as restful as a wasp.

Wings in full flurry. The blur compels you
to stay in the tub.
I let myself be drained.

Those visible capillaries are a warning that your skin is no longer yours –

keep your damn fingers out of your mouth. Put socks on
your hands and suck your own
spit back. Wrong pipe, same diff.

When my doctor says, *Wow, you were aggressive*
I'm more flattered than is sensible.
I've always known how to burn away my body

and pick myself for pain, no gain no heal, you know
how they say that, how I say that, burning
all my excess off. I change the dressing three times a day

religiously. Like a growth is a god and cleanliness
is a virtue. My mouth is an altar that creates its own rain.
I lick the fluids before I realize what I'm doing.

That counts right? I'm more scar tissue than not
so accept it – raised edges, discoloration. Pain must
match the rate of growth.

So burn it.
Pray. Then,
start again.

Grieving, year 15

I had a great day at work today
My mom's hands were soft

On the drive home I wept
trying to remember

just moments ago
the famous old author's soft hands

on my wrist on my arm
trying to remember

Circling

I thought I saw a loon nesting on that island
in between the tufts of grass, but
I don't trust what I see most days
so, let's circle around again.

It's hard to tell if she's belly up or
guarding the nest when we drift by.

Circle round, let me

steer, slow
ripple, fade.

Her red eye
finds us.

I thought I saw the hillside of trees breathe in unison
this morning. I thought I saw a dog
swimming but it was two young deer, bounding away without
shaking off. I thought I saw a spider the size of my hand
as I sat on the dock, but convinced myself it was only cracked paint

on the old canoe's bottom,
black legs on white, are they
                                        moving?

Is it me?
But
                        it actually was a spider –

I only trusted myself
when you saw it too.

I thought I saw my mom
step around a corner for years.

It's hard to tell
if she's belly up or
guarding me, hard
to know
the difference

between haunted and protected, but you know it when
you see it –

a horsefly lands and leaves just as
          the sandal drops.

I thought I
hit him, thought
I saw

the
body
a
trick
of
light

rocks
slick with moss   sometimes
a fish   sometimes
nothing   othertimes

a delicate collection of all
the leaves a forest does away with now

settled circle by if you're still

circle by if you're not

belly up circle by protect me.

I thought I heard a fly this morning

buzzing smack
into the window,
over and over, but

it was actually a wasp.
We made a puzzle of glass and screens
for it to figure through, point home.

That night it was belly up
on the nightstand by my ChapStick, head curled
sad toward its stinger.

Did you see?

I folded the body
            gently

into two tissues
the way my mommy taught me.
I didn't crush it. I learned.
I still have the scar, see?

Wait – I don't. I could have
sworn I could see it.
Let's circle around again.

Do you see it?
That loon nesting?
Obscured by low bushes?

Do you see it?
Did you see her too?

//

Standing in our name

I've
wanted

many things

little

tension

a lake

wanting

to express it

believe
in –

wanting

a body

a life

My voice

my voice

my voice

her eyes understand

Her mind

Her body

my eyes

her legs

Her voice her back

her voice is gone,

and mine. Her body

her aura

my body her,

blood

her head. My head her head her aura mine

My lungs

her soft hands,

my face

Our hurt

Our voice

our kneeling our skin. My voice

Every day. Water droplets on my edges. I dab my face with oil, shove Vaseline into my nostrils. Every day. I want to erase some years. Kneeling pain. Water wanting. A clear vision of leaves looking through the dry window. A lake with no water and me at the centre kneeling wanting nothing. Water nothing. Kneeling leaves. Pointing. What do you want? What is your name?

A small gift like a prayer given to me in ink. A cold window. A warm want. Our name once gave me nothing but want and refusal but concession but connection and connection is the window of wanting I want to look through the lake I want to stand in the water I wish to drown in but I wipe it off instead.

she picked me up,

I picked her up,

she said

love
love
love

every day.

here right here,
still

NOTES

The quote at the start of "Kneeling" is taken from *Third-Millennium Heart* by Ursula Andkjær Olsen, translated by Katrine Øgaard Jensen. The "red" imagery throughout that section and this book was jump-started by inspiration from *Third-Millenium Heart*.

The quote at the start of "Floating" is taken from *Big Shadow* (Book*hug Press, 2023) by Marta Balcewicz.

The quote at the start of "Standing" is taken from Hanif Abdurraqib's *There's Always This Year* (Penguin Random House, 2024).

"My little sister asks me" was inspired by a prose poem by Sanna Wani called "Lately I Am Trying," published in *Ex/Post* magazine in January 2022.

"Marble People" was inspired after sitting on the porch one morning, drinking coffee, reading Mary Ruefle's "A Morning Person" (*Poetry Review* 109, no. 2 [summer 2019]). It plays off the last line in her poem: "I hate my poems."

"Floating in Our Name" and "Standing in Our Name" are made up of de/reconstructions of lines and/or erasures from "Kneeling in Our Name."

ACKNOWLEDGEMENTS

I want to say a little bit more about my mommy, Sharon Conyer. She has three daughters – Cat, me and Page – and she loved us with all her heart, and she loves us still. I feel it every day. Every day. We love her and miss her every day, too. Our mom had a beautiful singing voice and she loved the bell choir and she loved Halloween, when she almost always would dress as a witch and decorate the house with plastic rats. Our mom was a goofball; she sang silly songs. She had the most generous heart. She was extremely short and lied about being five feet tall – she totally wasn't. She stood up to teachers or coaches who were mean to us; sometimes those teachers ended up apologizing to *us* after she was done with them. We always knew she had our backs. She was born in Western Kentucky and her accent was amazing, she loved New Orleans, she was a great friend who would kill for you. When she was mad at us, she gave us the stink eye, but it just made us laugh because it looked so damn ridiculous. When we were mad at her, to make *us* laugh, she made us recite: "My mommy is the best mommy in the whoooole wiiiiide world." She was. She is.

—

Thank you so much to the journals, magazines and chapbook presses that published previous versions of some of these poems:

ALOCASIA, no, 1 (June 2022): "Today I put my hands into dirt, and it was warm"

Anti-Heroin Chic (February 2019): "Replacement therapy"

Canthius, no. 10 (Summer 2022): "In the box of jewellery we went through when our mother died"

carte blanche, no. 42, Disability Themed issue (December 2021): "Chaudière Falls"

Contemporary Verse 2 44, no. 4, Sick Poetics issue (Spring 2022): "Those visible capillaries are a warning sign that your skin is no longer yours –" and "I don't know how it's possible"

Contemporary Verse 2 44, no. 2 (Fall 2021): "Close your eyes so you can see"

Decameron Series: A version of "The mirror"

Gap Riot Press, Season 10 (2024): "Kneeling in our name" as a chapbook.

The Minola Review (October 2020): "You never touched me in public," now titled "Who walks away clean"

Non.Plus Lit, no. 2 (October 2020): "Google Doc of Death"

Parentheses Journal, no. 8 (Winter 2020): "Only for so long," which became "A fly lands on the window"

periodicities, prose poem folio (March 2022): "My little sister asks me"

Pinhole Poetry 1, no. 2 (July 2022): "Restful as a hornet," now titled "Restful as a wasp"

Puddles of Sky Postcard #1 (February 2018): "Cloud cover"

The Quarantine Review, no. 8 (Summer 2021): "grieving, year 10" (from "Perennial")

Sawdust Reading Series 4th Anniversary Collection 2017–2018, and *If the river stood still* (Audio Recording/Album, 2018): "Encasement"

Watch Your Head (June 2022): "Ripple"

—

Huge gratitude to the MacDowell Foundation for the time and beautiful surroundings that allowed me to, along with other projects, work on completing the final edits of this book in summer 2025.

Massive thanks as well to the Ontario Arts Council for the Recommender Grants Program for funding this project, specifically to recommenders *Arc Poetry Magazine*, Invisible Publishing and Brick Books for recommending an early version of this manuscript for funding.

Thank you as well to the City of Ottawa Arts Funding Program for funding this project.

Dani Spinosa and Kate Siklosi of Gap Riot: Thank you for believing in *Kneeling in Our Name* as a chapbook. I was in a sad state, feeling pretty down on myself as an artist when I got the news that you wanted to publish it, and it really picked me up. Thank you so much. Gap Riot rules.

To all my friends, creative peers and loved ones who make life and art less lonely and more inspiring, I love you! Page Conyer, Cat Gallagher, Manahil Bandukwala, Edwin Ramirez, Margo LaPierre, Kelli Kessling, Ellen Chang-Richardson, Chris Johnson, nina jane drystek, Nathanael

Larochette, Mahaila Smith, Helen Robertson, Dave Currie, Sanna Wani, Stuart Ross, Khashayar "Kess" Mohammadi, Terese Mason Pierre, Liam Burke, Natalie Hanna, Gary Barwin, and many many many more people who now are probably mad at me because I didn't explicitly list them and this is deeply anxiety producing, oh god.

The entire Perfect Books crew: My wonderful indie bookstore people, what can I say? I appreciate you all so much. I love talking about art and laughing with you all. SUPPORT INDEPENDENT BOOKSTORES!

Chelsea Harlan: I am so grateful to have spent a wonderful, surreally gorgeous week together at MacDowell, sharing in art, looking at deer, swimming and performing poetry together. Thank you endlessly for blurbing my book! You are the best.

Cassidy McFadzean: I am so glad to have connected with you nearly five years ago, as I am writing this, despite it being through grief, and to now call you my friend. Your endorsement on this book means so much to me. I admire you in so many ways – your art, your activism, your honesty. Thank you, pal.

Mikko Harvey: I am such a fan and am so delighted and honoured you were willing to give a blurb for this book. Your work touches my heart in a truly singular, aching, magical way; it is something I aim for. Thank you!

Natasha Ramoutar: You were the best editor for this collection I could have possibly asked for. I cannot thank you enough for your patience, care and guidance as we talked about this book. I appreciate everything you've done to make this book what it is.

To everyone at Buckrider Books / Wolsak and Wynn: Paul Vermeersch, Noelle Allen, Natasha Ramoutar, Ashley Hisson, Jen Rawlinson and cover designer Natalie Olsen, you are truly the best! Thank you for bringing me onto the W&W team. I am so happy to be here!

—

I like reading about grief while grieving (always grieving). Maybe you are grieving, too. Thank you for reading.

CONYER CLAYTON is a queer writer and editor from Louisville, a dual US-Canadian citizen living between Ottawa and Kentucky. They are the author of *But the sun, and the ships, and the fish, and the waves* (Winner of the Archibald Lampman Award), *We Shed Our Skin Like Dynamite* (Winner of the Ottawa Book Award) and many chapbooks. Conyer's fiction has been supported by a MacDowell Fellowship, a McCormack Writing Center Scholarship and the Canada Council for the Arts. *the lake-shaped excuse* is their third book.